Arthur Ransome's Lakeland

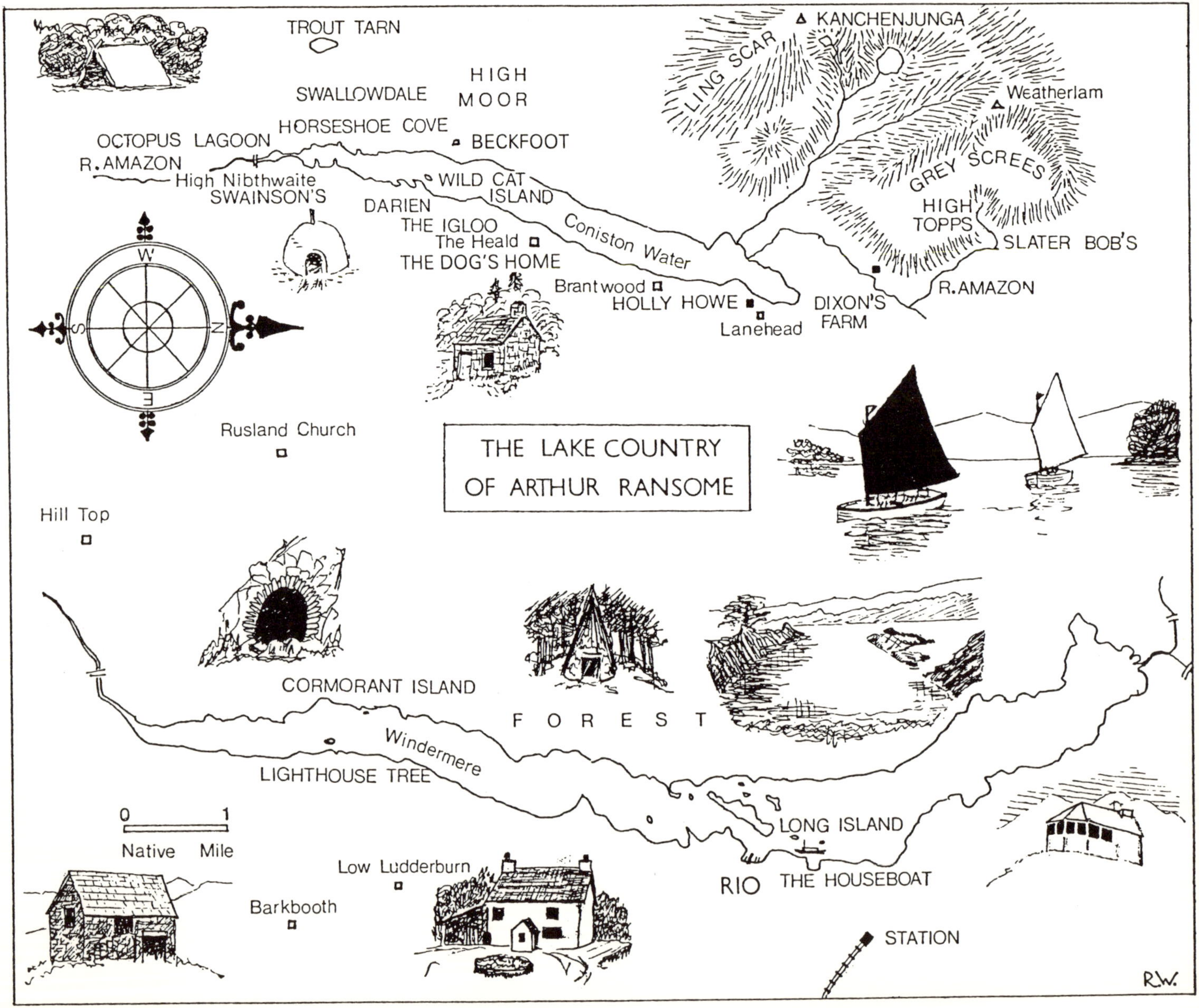

THE LAKE COUNTRY OF ARTHUR RANSOME
TROUT TARN
KANCHENJUNGA
LING SCAR
Weatherlam
HIGH MOOR
SWALLOWDALE
HORSESHOE COVE
OCTOPUS LAGOON
BECKFOOT
R. AMAZON
High Nibthwaite
SWAINSON'S
WILD CAT ISLAND
GREY SCREES
DARIEN
HIGH TOPPS
THE IGLOO
Coniston Water
The Heald
SLATER BOB'S
THE DOG'S HOME
Brantwood
R. AMAZON
HOLLY HOWE
DIXON'S FARM
Lanehead
W
S
N
E
Rusland Church
Hill Top
CORMORANT ISLAND
FOREST
Windermere
LIGHTHOUSE TREE
LONG ISLAND
0
1
Native Mile
Low Ludderburn
RIO
THE HOUSEBOAT
Barkbooth
STATION
R.W.

Arthur Ransome's Lakeland

A quest for the real "Swallows and Amazons" country

by Roger Wardale

with extracts from the original stories by Arthur Ransome

Dalesman Books 1988

The Dalesman Publishing Company Ltd.,
Clapham, Lancaster, LA2 8EB.
First published 1986
Second edition 1988

ISBN: 0 85206 930 8

Dedicated to my mother who started it all

Printed in Great Britain by Fretwell & Cox Ltd.,
Goulbourne Street, Keighley, West Yorkshire BD21 1PZ.

Contents

Cover photograph:
Ransome country seen through the trees of the Peak in Darien. Dominating the skyline beyond High Moor is Kanchenjunga. The rocks on the right give shelter to the secret harbours of Wild Cat Island. (Photo: Tom Parker).

The only way to keep
a secret (your own
or other people's) is
NEVER to answer
a question. But you
seem good at guessing.
All the places in the
books are to be found,
but not arranged quite
as in the ordnance maps.
You seem to be just
the reader for these books.
I am glad you like
them.
With best wishes from
Arthur Ransome

The letter from Arthur Ransome to the author which started the quest.

Introduction

I looked out of the shelter where I was sitting into the gloom of a wet August Sunday morning and was blissfully happy. The rain beat on the roof of the shelter and from time to time it splashed bubbles on the surface of the lake. I looked across the grey lake to the grey trees on the island and beyond. After years of waiting I was in Rio Bay at last! I had persuaded my mother to bring me on the nine-hour train journey from the South Coast to stay in Bowness for a week and we had arrived in drizzle only the evening before. The boatsheds where *Swallow* was repaired stood at the water's edge, just where I had expected. Every now and then a steamer called at the pier, just as I knew it would. Out on the lake yachts bobbed at their moorings and away behind the pier stood the hotel where Squashy Hat had a friend who supplied him with food. It was all quite perfect and the weather did not matter at all.

A few days later we were walking along Rayrigg Road, just north of the bay, when we came to another bay. In this bay, lying a short distance from the shore, was the houseboat. I had looked at the drawing in *Swallowdale* too many times not to recognise it instantly. I lost no time in taking a photograph. I half expected a large man with a bald head to appear from out of the cabin. We did not have very good weather that week, but I saw enough to realise that the setting of Arthur Ransome's books was all around me and that the places were almost certainly there somewhere, waiting to be discovered.

Greatly daring, I wrote to Arthur Ransome to tell him what I had seen and ask him to confirm that Bowness was Rio, the houseboat was now moored in Rayrigg Bay and that he was Captain Flint, as a photograph I had seen seemed to suggest. More importantly, I wanted to return and discover more, so please would he tell me where I could find the other places. He replied with the sort of letter he must have written dozens of times to young admirers.

> The only way to keep a secret (your own and other people's) is NEVER to answer a question. But you seem good at guessing. All the places in the books are to be found, but not arranged quite as in the ordnance maps. You seem to be just the reader for those books. I am glad you like them.
>
> With best wishes from
>
> Arthur Ransome

"All the places are to be found . . . " Arthur Ransome could not have written anything more exciting. I felt as if he approved of my quest, had told me enough to set me looking and challenged me to find them for myself. I made up my mind to accept the challenge and resolved that, with books, maps and journeys north when I could do so, I would find all the places and photograph them as I had done the houseboat. That was thirty years ago. It has been great fun and given a purpose to many a Lakeland expedition. The result of my exploration is this book.

Before I was able to read them for myself I heard "Uncle Mac" read *"The Big Six"* on Children's Hour during the war. Soon afterwards my mother was sent to the public library in search of more. When she found one she returned to the library at fortnightly intervals to have it renewed or occasionally exchanged for another. After the war the paper shortage continued and as the books re-appeared in the bookshops they were bought on sight and kept until the next birthday or Christmas. If it was one I had not read I was allowed one peep at the pictures.

My first hunt for the lake was among the maps of M.J.B. Baddeley's *The English Lake District*. It took me a long time to decide that Windermere was the most likely, because although the islands off Rio seemed to fit in, the lake was too long and narrow, and the River Amazon was missing completely. In the end we decided to stay in Bowness because there was plenty of accommodation and it might turn out to be Rio.

It was W.G. Collingwood, Arthur's great friend and mentor, who gave away the secret of Wild Cat Island. I found his book *The Lake Counties* in the library and in the chapter on Coniston Water he mentions Peel Island. He describes the island in detail, with its mass of bluebells in spring and bell-heather in summer, for he knew the place well. He adds that readers of the recent books by Arthur Ransome will recognise the place, because the island has only been altered a little by literary camouflage and all its charm has been preserved.

Much later I came across a letter published in a pre-war *Junior Bookshelf* in which Arthur himself lets out some secrets. He explains that Bowness is Rio, the lake is Windermere and that Cormorant Island is Silver Holme. He admits that lots of people had discovered that Kanchenjunga is Coniston Old Man. I have taken more than five hundred children up Kanchenjunga. The climb is the climax of a week spent in Ransome's Lakeland on an Educational Visit. They never fail to respond to the grandeur of the mountains, so very different to the country where they live and they search eagerly through binoculars for Wild Cat Island as they stand by the summit cairn.

I found Octopus Lagoon and the Amazon River after much studying of the 2½-inch ordnance maps. There is not much literary camouflage except that the River Crake flows out of Coniston Water instead of into it. It seems that the River Amazon is a composite of those becks and rivers he knew best. Yewdale Beck flows into the River Crake after being joined by the becks which drop from Low Water and Levers Water.

Four books have been invaluable. In 1969 came the autobiographical *In Aleppo Once* by Taqui Altounyan. She remembers how surprised and pleased they were to be put into a book by "Uncle Arthur". A little exploration around their old home at Lanehead revealed Holly Howe and the boathouse at the bottom of the field. In 1976 came the *Autobiography* and the beginning of the book tells with great clarity and affection of his early holidays by Coniston Water. Aspects of the district and incidents in his life which he wove so brilliantly into his stories are told for the first time. My quest gained added impetus with its publication. To mark the centenary of Arthur's birth, Hugh Brogan's *The Life of Arthur Ransome* was published. Not only does Hugh Brogan include details of Arthur's life which he had omitted from the Autobiography, but he also gives a fascinating insight into the way the books were written. Less than a year later came Christina Hardyment's *Arthur Ransome and Captain Flint's Trunk*. In a few months she had discovered almost all the Ransome sites in Lakeland, East Anglia and the Norfolk Broads. More than that she had burrowed into the Ransome archives at the University of Leeds and had further increased our knowledge of the way Arthur worked and the influences which resulted in the adventures of the Swallows and Amazons. The book ends with an extract from part of the unfinished thirteenth novel *Coots in the North*.

Finally, in 1985 I followed a beck as it wound its way through waist-high bracken and climbed up beside the waterfall, as Titty and Roger had done, to find myself in the secret valley of Swallowdale. It was a moment both sad and satisfying and it was entirely fitting that my discoveries should end in such a special place. A couple of days later I had tea with an Amazon and two Swallows, less than an arrow's flight from Swainson's Farm, the place where it had all started almost a hundred years before. Down in the bay by the boathouse children and grandchildren were aboard the *Amazon* and a native war canoe, and there had been talk of spending a night on Wild Cat Island. My quest could not have had a better finale.

Arthur Ransome

Arthur Ransome was born in Leeds in 1884. He was still a baby when his father brought him to the Lake District and carried him up to the summit of Coniston Old Man. His father was Professor of History at the Yorkshire College (now the University of Leeds), but he was a countryman at heart with a passion for the Lake District. Arthur was soon to share that passion. From about the age of seven, until his father's death in 1897, he spent the long summer holidays at Swainson's Farm in High Nibthwaite near the foot of Coniston Water, where the family stayed each year. Arthur told of his secret greeting of the lake whenever he had been away, as he dipped his hands into the water to prove to himself that he was really home. These were idyllic days, spent on the lake and among the gentle fells and woods nearby, making friends with the local people and joining in their traditional way of life. While their father fished and their mother painted in water-colours, Arthur and his brother and sisters were, in his own words, "Free in paradise". Sometimes they would row a mile up the lake to a little rocky, wooded island where they picnicked, while his father drifted along by the shore fishing for trout. This world of rocks, heather, bracken, tinkling becks and drystone walls, inhabited by a wealth of wildlife, charcoal burners, shepherds and gamekeepers was the one he returned to again and again throughout his life.

He was a lively, sensitive and rather naughty small boy. When he was nine he was sent to prep schol at the Old College in Windermere. Here because of his short-sight and resultant failure at boxing and other sports he was called a coward and became the butt of boys and staff alike. He was intensely miserable at the school, except for a few weeks during the great frost of 1895 when Windermere froze from end to end and the boys spent whole days on the ice.

His father's death, following a fall whilst fishing, occurred just before he went to Rugby and brought an end to the Nibthwaite holidays. At Rugby his short sight was discovered and immediately corrected with spectacles and Arthur began to enjoy school life. He even managed to play for his house fifteen. It was during his time at Rugby that he was encouraged to consider writing as a career, much to the dismay of his mother who wanted her elder son to settle down to a good, steady job. From Rugby he went to the Yorkshire College to read science.

After less than two terms he managed to persuade his mother to let him go to London as a publisher's office-boy. In his spare time he began writing for magazines and as soon as he could afford to do so, he hurried north to Coniston to continue his Lakeland holidays. Here he met the artist and writer W.G. Collingwood. Arthur's friendship with his adopted "aunt" and "uncle" and their family was the most important of his life. They gave him the support and inspiration he had failed to find in his own family. In his biography which Arthur wrote partly to express his debt, he says the rest of his life was happier because of them. The Collingwoods lived at Lanehead, near the head of Coniston Water. Arthur's idyllic Lakeland holidays continued in their company.

Dora and Barbara were about the same age as Arthur and they were ideal companions. After a morning devoted to writing and painting they would sail away and picnic. It was the Collingwoods who taught Arthur to sail, just as his father had taught him to fish. Sometimes they sailed down the lake to picnic on the same island of his Nibthwaite holidays. It was hardly surprising that he fell in love with Barbara, who took a long time to make up her mind, but finally refused him. They remained friends for life.

He kept a steady job in publishing for less than two years. Encouraged by the sale of stories and articles to magazines and with the moral support of the Collingwoods, he began his life as a man of letters. He managed to scrape a living from his writing until his first book was published in 1907. This was a collection of essays on artistic life in the capital, *Bohemia in London*. It was Arthur's first success. After Barbara's rejection he spent the next three summers at Wall Nook Farm, near Cartmel. Here he worked and walked and learned to wrestle Cumberland and Westmorland style. The following year he was back at Coniston at Low Yewdale, just above the head of the lake. In fine weather he camped out and he continued to be a frequent visitor at Lanehead. The younger Collingwoods, Robin and Ursula, were old enough to be good company too and it was with Robin that he enoyed spirited single-handed dinghy races on the lake.

Although he was essentially a countryman, Arthur enjoyed his impoverished Bohemian life in London and it was at his Chelsea flat that he first met Ivy Constance Walker who succeeded in trapping him into marriage. Ivy was a woman of wild fantasies who censored Arthur's letters and made normal home life impossible. When their daughter Tabitha was born Arthur saw that she was christened in Coniston church, but it was not long before they were living in Wiltshire. He was very fond of Tabitha, but after a few years when Ivy refused to consider a divorce, he fled to Russia.

Arthur needed to get right away and in 1913 his plan to write a book of Russian fairy stories gave him a reason for going and the means to achieve his escape. Before long he became the Russian correspondent of the *Daily Chronicle*, having taught himself the language by racing through Russian children's readers. At the same time he was working on his book of fairy stories, and in 1916 *Old Peter's Russian Tales* was published and it has been reprinted many times since. In spite of the bad health which was to plague him for the rest of his life, he remained in Russia throughout the war and the Russian Revolution. He sent eye-witness accounts of the day to day happenings of the

Left: Nearly a hundred years have passed since Professor Ransome brought his family to stay at Swainson's Farm in High Nibthwaite for the long summer vacation, but it is easily recognisable from the *Autobiography*.

Opposite: Lanehead at the head of Coniston Water was the home of the Collingwoods until about twenty years ago. The time Arthur Ransome spent here with the family of artists and writers was of great importance to him.

Low Ludderburn, the Ransomes' tiny, four-roomed cottage at the head of the Cartmel valley which was their home for ten years from 1925.

Beside the cottage at Low Ludderburn stands a large barn. The Ransomes turned the upper floor into a workroom adding the window overlooking the valley and a fireplace. Awkward slate slabs lead to the workroom and both Arthur and Evgenia had falls. Here Arthur wrote *Swallows and Amazons,* taking the manuscript into his bedroom so as to touch it as he lay in bed.

The Heald with its seventeen acres and half a mile of lake-shore was the Ransomes' home during the second world war.

revolution to the *Daily News* and it was while he was gathering reports from the Bolshevics that he met and fell in love with Trotsky's secretary. She was the "tall, jolly girl", Evgenia Petrovna Shelepina, who was to become his second wife and sternest critic. His period in Russia reveals him as a brave and resourceful man with no interest in politics whatever. With his sprig of heather from Peel Island, he seems to have been passing time waiting for the opportunity to return to the Lake Country and his fishing.

For the next few years Arthur and Evgenia lived in Estonia. He was now writing for the *Manchester Guardian* and they took the opportunity to enjoy some sailing. Finally he had the famous *Racundra* built for them to cruise in the Baltic and this first voyage inspired one of the finest of all cruising yarns, *Racundra's First Cruise*. In 1924 he was free to marry Evgenia, Ivy having at last divorced him, and a year later they were house-hunting in Lakeland. They bought Low Ludderburn, a small, isolated cottage with a glorious view across the Winster Valley to Yorkshire forty miles away. In order to buy it they had, with great regret, to sell *Racundra,* but they had fallen in love with the place. They had ten happy years at Ludderburn. A large barn stands alongside the cottage and this was converted into a splendid workroom for Arthur. At first he continued with his articles for the *Manchester Guardian,* but he still hoped to be able to give up journalism for writing books. In 1929, with *Swallows and Amazons* unfinished, he found that he could not write essays and fiction at the same time. He realised he must choose between a regular income and that which he could produce by writing books. With Evgenia's support he decided to resign from the paper and work for them as a freelance only.

When *Swallows and Amazons* was completed, he waited

Left: Hill Top, Haverthwaite was the Ransomes' last home. Here they lived each summer from the early 1950s. Finally they bought the house and spent three years in the peaceful spot.

Right: Arthur Ransome (from a pencil sketch by the author).

impatiently for publication. He need not have worried for it was well received. Although it sold slowly he was sufficiently encouraged to start a sequel. At last, twenty-five years after *Bohemia in London,* he was able to write stories which he truly cared about and indulge in his twin pastimes of sailing and fishing. These were truly halcyon days for Arthur, marred only by periods of ill-health.

In 1935 the Ransomes left Ludderburn for East Anglia. Evgenia was finding the isolated cottage hard to run and they both wanted to continue the life they had lost with the sale of *Racundra.* They settled near Pin Mill and bought a seven-ton cutter which they re-named *Nancy Blackett.* They enjoyed their years on the East coast, but soon after the start of World War II the Ransomes were back in Lakeland.

They bought "The Heald" on the east side of Coniston Water, about a mile north of Peel Island. As well as the bungalow went seventeen acres including some lake frontage. A couple of years later *The Picts and the Martyrs* was published, much to the delight of his army of readers who had hoped for a return to the lake of his early stories. Unfortunately Evgenia was never happy at the bungalow for it was very isolated and when the war was over they sold it and moved to London.

In 1948 they were back in the lakes again, this time at Lowick Hall. The hall and nearby farm proved too much for them to run and after a couple of years they returned to London. They were able to enjoy sailing long after Arthur's doctors had told him to give it up. *Lottie Blossom,* their last boat, was kept in Chichester Harbour and they sailed her until 1954.

In 1951 the University of Leeds made him an honorary D.Litt. and in 1953 he received the CBE. In 1937 *Pigeon Post* had won the first Carnegie medal for the best children's book of the year.

He was now Dr. Ransome, spending his summers in the Lake country and the winters in London playing chess and billiards at the Garrick Club. In 1960 when Arthur was 76 they bought Hill Top, near Haverthwaite at the foot of Windermere. It was to be their last home. Arthur died seven years later and Evgenia a further seven after that. They lie buried in Rusland churchyard in a beautiful, peaceful valley in the heart of that corner of Lakeland he had made his own and brought to life so vividly in his books.

People and Places

The story of *Swallows and Amazons* began in 1928. Dora Collingwood had married Ernest Altounyan, another of Arthur's friends from his Lanehead days, and they had gone out to Aleppo in Syria where he helped his father run the hospital. Every few years they brought the children back to Lanehead to visit their grandparents. By 1928 their family was complete with Taqui, Susie, Mavis (known as Titty, Roger and Brigit.

Taqui became a writer and Titty, the artist of the family, lives in Coniston. Susie married a Frenchman and lives in France. Roger, after service as a pilot during World War II, qualified as a doctor and joined his father and grandfather in the hospital in Aleppo. His later career was devoted to asthma research. As a sufferer, he conducted experiments upon himself. The result was the Intal treatment and the spinhaler which have brought relief to millions of other sufferers throughout the world.

Soon after they had arrived for the summer in April, Ernest went to Barrow-in-Furness and bought two sturdy sailing dinghies for £15 each. These were delivered to Coniston by lorry and soon the children were learning to sail. It had been agreed that at the end of the summer one of the dinghies would become Arthur's, while the other would remain in the Altounyan's possession. Naturally Arthur joined in the sailing lessons and it must have been a memorable summer for all of them.

Taqui and Titty usually sailed the *Mavis*. She has a heavy iron centreboard and is thirteen feet long. She was built by McVey of Piel Island near Barrow about 1920. At various times she has had a white sail or a brown sail and is afloat in her boathouse at Nibthwaite to this day. Nowadays she has a "miner's wheel", as Taqui calls it, to assist in raising the centreboard. This was an addition of Oscar Gnosspelius, who made two appearances in the books as Squashy Hat. Some years ago Ernest had to sheath her in fibre-glass, but she is still very much her old self, beloved and sailed by three generations of the family.

Their other boat was the *Swallow* which was a little longer and roomier. She was built by Crossfields of Arnside and was usually sailed by Susie and Roger. She was fast and stable with a rather deep keel and a brown sail. She became the children's favourite and at the end of the summer, when they returned to Syria, they generously gave her to Arthur. Sadly, greatly to their surprise, he parted with her when they moved to Suffolk seven years later. I have not been able to find anyone who knows what became of her.

Swallows and Amazons was written for the Altounyan children after they had returned to Aleppo to remind them of the Lake Country. It was to be about their favourite boat, the *Swallow,* which he was sailing on Windermere. He thought of the days of his youth on Coniston Water and of Peel Island and quickly the story took shape in his mind. There were too many girls in the Altounyan family, so Arthur decided that the eldest should be a boy. John Walker was the capable, natural leader he would have liked to have been as a boy. His name may have been borrowed from a Bowness boatman. The green Victorian boatmen's huts had names over the doors and one of these was John Walker. It was there as recently as 1960, and if it had been there thirty years earlier Arthur would have seen it many times. Perhaps he knew the boatman himself. The other young Altounyans gave their names and something of themselves to the crew of the *Swallow*.

All Arthur ever said of the origin of the Amazon pirates was that he remembered seeing two small girls playing by the lake shore wearing red caps. It is probable that Taqui Altounyan was partly the model for Nancy without ever realising it. She was the elder sailor on the *Mavis* which appeared in the story as the *Amazon* and was nearly the right age. She has always been more adventurous than the rest of the family and as the eldest would have made an impression on Arthur, who was as capable of changing families to suit the needs of the story as he was of moving rivers. In her delightful book of childhood memories *In Aleppo Once,* Taqui reveals herself as a perceptive young

Roger aged about eight. A painting by his mother Dora Altounyan. (Photo: Brigit Sanders)

lady of strong character — rather like Nancy Blackett. She was never allowed to think of herself as Captain Nancy however, but meeting her more than fifty years later I am more than half convinced.

There are other possible "originals" for the Blacketts. Pauline and Georgina Rawdon-Smith were a couple of tomboys who stayed at Tent Lodge, next to Lanehead. They only met the Ransomes on one occasion, but became sure that they were the Amazon pirates. Whatever her origin, Nancy became very real to Arthur, like the other characters he developed, and these in turn have become real to three generations of readers.

At Abbot Hall Museum I came across a sheet on which were the names and ages of the characters. Nancy was 13, John and Peggy 12, Susan 10, Titty 9, Roger 7 and Vicky (Bridget) 1½. For part of their summer holidays they stay in a farm by the lake. The lake is very like Windermere, but is a little wider and not quite so long. Part of it comes from Coniston Water. The farm was the one the Altounyans knew well, because it is just below Lanehead. Bank Ground Farm looks just like the illustration in *Swallowdale*. The field slopes down to the lake, where there are boathouses and a jetty. Darien is nowhere to be seen, but there are several tree-covered cliffs on Windermere and Coniston. Friar's Crag, away on Derwentwater, looks just right, however, I believe the idea comes from the cliffs at High Peel Near, just up the road from Nibthwaite and overlooking Peel Island. Here the young Arthur may well have looked across the lake in anticipation.

After receiving a telegram of approval from their father in the best Ernest Altounyan manner, the children are allowed to sail to the nearby island while Mother, Vicky and Nurse remain at Holly Howe Farm. Arthur has said at different times that the island was mainly Peel Island, that it was mainly Blake Holme on Windermere and that it was a mixture of the two. I believe that Wild Cat Island is essentially Peel Island. It was the happy picnic spot of his childhood and as a young man he had camped there. For the Collingwoods and Altounyans as well as for himself it was a very special place. Then there is the evidence of W.G. Collingwood in *The Lake Counties,* who would have known as much about it as anyone. But most of all, it has the secret harbour. The lighthouse tree has certainly been borrowed from Blake Holme, which has several to spare.

On their voyage of discovery the children see the houseboat. I am sure this was the *Esperance* I saw in Rayrigg Bay all those years ago. Arthur once altered a postcard of the *Gondola* on Coniston to look "something like" the houseboat, probably because he had no postcard of *Esperance* at the time. The drawings look like *Esperance,* which is not surprising because at the Windermere Steamboat Museum, where she is now on show, they told me that Bowness boatmen remembered him sitting down in Bowness Bay to draw her. Another feature in her favour is the narrow gangway beside the cabin mentioned twice in the story which the *Gondola* does not possess.

Just across the bay from the island is Dixon's Farm where they collect the morning milk. This is modelled on Low Yewdale Farm where he stayed one year. After a few days of gentle exploring and fishing comes the famous meeting with the Amazon pirates. It is the relationship between the Swallows and their uncle, who owns the houseboat, which forms one of the main themes of the story. This is Arthur Ransome himself, thinly disguised by a different pirate past and known as Captain Flint. Soon the Swallows and Amazons are allies, on the best of terms — and at war. The Amazons live at the north end of the lake beyond the islands. Bowness and its islands have become Rio and its islands, and the picture of this part of the lake is particularly accurate. Their home is Beckfoot by the River Amazon, downstream from the Octupus Lagoon, the scene of the Swallow's unsuccessful cutting-out expedition in the dark. This is the River Crake and Allen Tarn, while Beckfoot itself lies at the mouth of Torver Beck, across the lake from Peel Island. There is a large house near Low Nibthwaite, which is in relatively the right area, and Tent Lodge, the holiday home of the Rawdon-Smiths, looks a little like the drawings.

During that night of high adventure Titty captures the *Amazon* by accident and overhears burglars burying a trunk they have stolen from the houseboat on Cormorant Island. Its recovery and return to Captain Flint leads to a reconciliation and the Swallows' holiday ends with them sharing the camp on Wild Cat Island with the Amazons, who have a tent with ears, like Arthur's own.

In the background of the story, the life of the lake is

always there, with its public steamers, launches, yachts, fishermen and rowing boats all regarded as native craft.

The story continues the following August in *Swallowdale*. Shortly after they arrive, John wrecks the *Swallow* off Horseshoe Cove in a manner similar to an accident Arthur had himself. While *Swallow* is repaired they are confined to dry land. Horseshoe Cove lies on the opposite side of the lake to Nibthwaite. The children camp in a beautiful secret valley, shut in with rocks and a waterfall at each end. This is also at the south end of Coniston Water. Swallowdale has its own knickerbockerbreaker down which Roger slides, but the idea comes from childhood days when Arthur slid down rocks at the back of Swainson's Farm and was darned by Annie Swainson who becomes Mary Swainson when she darns Roger. The farm is moved across the lake to provide the essential milk and supplies.

The misfortune with *Swallow* provides an opportunity to present a fascinating portrait of traditional Lakeland life. Farmers, charcoal burners and woodmen play their part, and a hound trail passes through the valley while the Swallows are there. Roger hears about the Grasmere Sports and wrestling from the old charcoal burner with whom he spends a night.

The Amazons and Captain Flint have worse problems with the visit to Beckfoot of the Great Aunt. They appear at intervals and on one occasion Captain Flint introduces John and Susan to the art of fly-fishing in Beacon Tarn, which is known as Trout Tarn. The distant peak of Kanchenjunga dominates the view across the moors from Swallowdale and before long they are planning to climb it. After a journey across High Moor the allies meet and row up the River Amazon until they meet the stream going down from Kanchenjunga. This is the beck which comes down Coppermines Valley from Low Water and Levers Water. The Swallows climb up the gorge and near the head of Coppermines Valley make their half-way camp.

The following day the Swallows and Amazons celebrate the departure of the Great Aunt by reaching the summit. The portrait of Coniston Old Man is quite an accurate one with the ridge where Roger saw the wild goats sweeping round to Brimfell. What a pity the explorers failed to notice the lovely tarns!

Later that day they encounter a thick fog and *Amazon* makes a memorable voyage through the islands to Horseshoe Cove. The Hen and Chicken rocks are moved into Rio Bay to provide an additional hazard.

Idyllic days return as the book ends and they are back on Wild Cat Island.

Winter Holiday takes place after the following Christmas. It introduces two delightful new characters. Dick and Dorothea Callum have no originals as such, but reflect two sides of Arthur's own character as a boy. The scientific Dick with his pre-occupation with the enthusiasm of the moment, and his elder sister Dorothea with her romantic vision and writer's vocation, are staying at Dixon's Farm.

Soon they meet the others and are invited to join the North Polar Expedition. They receive their instructions for the day from Holly Howe by means of the same signalling system he was using to signal to his friend Colonel Kelsall at Barkbooth, a mile across the valley from Low Ludderburn. I visited the fine old barn at Barkbooth and opened the small winnowing window to look out across a sea of tree tops to Low Ludderburn and the end wall, where the square and triangle indicated an important fishing message. From his barn Colonel Kelsall would reply.

The book owes much to the happy month Arthur spent during the Great Frost of 1895 at Windermere, when the lake froze from end to end. This happens during only the hardest of winters, about every thirty years. At least one incident came from real life. While he was busy with the story he went skating with Taqui, Susie and Titty at Tarn Hows. He recalls how Taqui and Susie were getting on pretty fast and that Titty was kicking herself along. By contrast the D's were more than competent skaters.

When Nancy's mumps provides the others with an extra month's holiday they are able to take advantage of the long freeze and make sledge journeys over the Arctic ice and turn the vacant houseboat into their own *Fram* as a base for the expedition. The head of the lake, referred to in the earlier books vaguely as the Arctic, becomes recognisable as the head of Windermere. The road running round the head of the lake is omitted so there is a clear run off the ice to the North Pole, a sort of summerhouse. One of the large houses at the head of the lake used to have such an addition, but it was removed some years ago.

The underlying theme of the book is the Ds' intense desire to be approved of by the others, especially Nancy. As town children they are out of their element and have to respond to unfamiliar situations. They eventually reach the North Pole in a blizzard, after Nancy forgets the original meaning of her trans-lake signal and they set off before the others. Throughout the book there is the background of the Lakes in a hard winter with its diversions and problems.

Next August Titty and Roger arrive by train at Strickland Junction (Oxenholme) to find a pigeon basket awaiting collection. After releasing the pigeon they continue their journey to Windermere. At the station they are met by Nancy and her mother in Rattletrap. This was probably Arthur's Trojan, for which he built a garage on the end of the barn at Low Ludderburn. At Beckfoot they find the others camped in the garden and full of plans to look for gold on the fells to keep the globe-trotting Captain Flint from being away in the holidays.

First they visit Slater Bob in his mine on the slopes of Kanchenjunga. This was John William Shaw and the mine was Penny Rigg Quarry where he worked. Slater Bob sends them to High Topps in search of gold. This is Yewdale Fells to the south-east of Wetherlam. Yewdale Beck and the road to Tilberthwaite forms the setting for the upper reaches of the River Amazon along which the mining company trek to Tyson's Farm so as to be near their work. There follows a systematic search of High Topps hampered by the presence of Squashy Hat who is looking for copper for his friend Captain Flint, unaware he has been mistaken for a rival gold-hunter. Squashy Hat was Oscar Gnosspelius, who had married Barbara Collingwood. He took Arthur to the Tilberthwaite mine and instructed him in mining so that the book should be accurate. Several different children had posed for the illustrations, and for the drawing of Nancy with the crushing mill, Janet, Oscar's daughter, posed with her father's pestle and mortar.

There is plenty of action and some danger before the mining company end up fighting a fell fire and discover that their gold is copper, which was what Squashy Hat, revealed as an ally, has been after all the time.

There are no new settings in *The Picts and the Martyrs* except for the hut in the wood where the D's stay in secret to prevent the Great Aunt from discovering Mrs. Blackett has invited them while Nancy and Peggy are alone at Beckfoot. Once again Arthur introduces a boat he owns. *Coch-y-bonddhu* was built by the boatbuilders who had built *Swallow* and was sailed in East Anglia and on Coniston Water. She become the *Scarab* which is built in Rio for Dick and Dorothea. When the Ransomes moved south at the end of the war she was sold and as far as I know her fate is unknown.

Nancy, in particular, carries the whole thing off splendidly and the Great Aunt returns mollified and impressed. The book ends with Captin Flint and Mrs. Blackett returning the following day, the Swallows due in a few days and five weeks of the holiday remaining. And that, for forty years, was that.

Then Hugh Brogan revealed that Abbot Hall Museum have an incomplete unpublished draft of the story he called *Coots in the North*. Joe, Bill and Pete stow away on a cruiser built in Horning, which is taken by road to Rio. When they arrive in Rio they start to look for the D's at Dixon's Farm. They are lent a dinghy by the cruiser's owner and set sail. On the lake they are spotted by the D's aboard *Scarab*, the Swallows are in close attendance and they meet Nancy in unexpected circumstances . . . .

The photographs and quotations on pages 22 to 61 are grouped in the same order as the books, beginning with *Swallows and Amazons* (1930) and ending with the unfinished *Coots in the North.*

Holly Howe

Roger, aged seven, and no longer the youngest of the family, ran in wide zigzags, to and fro across the steep field that sloped up from the lake to Holly Howe, the farm where they were staying for part of the summer hoidays.

Swallows and Amazons

Fishing for Char

Here and there, close to the shore, there were rowing boats with fishermen.

Swallows and Amazons

Darien

On the very evening of their first coming, a fortnight before, the children had found their way through the trees to the far end of the promontory, where it dropped, like a cliff, into the lake.

Swallows and Amazons

Wild Cat Island

Slowly the fleet slipped past Wild Cat Island. The island was once more the uninhabited island that Titty had watched for so many days from the Peak of Darien.

Swallows and Amazons

The Landing Place

John steered to pass between the island and the mainland, not too near the island so as not to lose wind. A little more than a third of the way along the eastern shore of the island there was a bay, a very small one, with a pebbly beach.

Swallows and Amazons

(Looking across the narrow channel to Peel Island the features of the island can be clearly seen).

The Secret Harbour

"What a place," said the able-seaman. "I expect somebody hid on the island hundreds of years ago, and kept his boat here."
"It's the perfect harbour," said John.

Swallows and Amazons

(Photo: Brigit Sanders)

Rio

The little town is called in the guide books by another name, but the crew of the ***Swallow*** *had long ago given it the name Rio Grande.*

Swallows and Amazons

The Houseboat

In the bay beyond the cape lay a strange-looking dark blue vessel. She was a long narrow craft with a high raised cabin roof, and a row of glass windows along her side. Her bows were like that of an old-time clipper. Her stern was like that of a steamship.

Swallows and Amazons

Arthur Ransome sailing Swallow

*Three or four short tacks brought the **Swallow** to the nearest of the landing stages for rowing boats that ran out from the shore in Rio Bay.*

Swallows and Amazons

Charcoal burning

A big puff of smoke rolled from the burning mound.
"Look there," said Young Billy. "Can't leave him a minute but he's out. Like the adder is fire. Just a bit of a hole and out he comes."

Swallows and Amazons

(A charcoal burn at Brantwood in 1985).

Octopus Lagoon

Suddenly the river broadened into a wide, open pool, with tall reeds all round it, except where the river entered and left it.
"This must be what they call the lagoon," said Captain John.

Swallows and Amazons

Cormorant Island

But there was nothing to be seen on the island, except the bare tree and the white splashed rocks and jetsom from the last flood, and big loose stones. They looked everywhere, Captain Flint climbed round the island two or three times. He could find nothing.

Swallows and Amazons

The Houseboat

*Able-seaman Titty was already running along the narrow gangway outside the cabin. In another moment, the huge elephant flag came fluttering down on the fore-deck.
"We've won," shouted John. "Your flag is struck."*

Swallows and Amazons

Horseshoe Cove

*The **Amazon** headed into a little bay on the western shore of the lake. The **Swallow** followed her. There were woods all round the little bay and a small stream ran into it. The Swallows and Amazons landed close by the mouth of the stream.*

Swallows and Amazons

The Lake looking south

The little brown-sailed ***Swallow*** *with her crew of five, including the parrot, had left Holly Howe Bay, and was now beating across the open lake that stretched away to the south between wooded hills.*

Swallowdale

The way to Swallowdale

She hurried forward again along a sheep track that led through the heather close above the stream. The boy ate a piece of chocolate he had saved, and hurried after the able-seaman. Sometimes the bracken grew so high they could hardly see each other.

Swallowdale

The entrance to Swallowdale

They hurried on until they stood below the waterfall. Above them the water poured down noisily from ledge to ledge of rock, and they could go no further without climbing up the rocks beside the falling water or getting out of the long winding gully that the stream had carved for itself in the moor.

Swallowdale

Swallowdale

She looked at the valley itself, and its steep sides, one of them on the right, almost a precipice of rock, with heather growing in the cracks of it, and the other, on the left, not so steep, with grass on it, bracken and loose stones.

Swallowdale

The Cave

He came running and found her looking under a clump of heather into a dark hole in the wall of grey rock.

Swallowdale

The Boatsheds

All along this nearer side of Rio Bay were the building yards.

Swallowdale

(These Victorian boatsheds were pulled down about 1973).

The Boatsheds

There were sheds a few yards back from the water, with railway lines running down into the lake.

Swallowdale

Lakeland Road

John had seen close in front of him a different wall . . . he guessed at once that the road must lie on the other side of it. At a place where a big copper beech spread its branches over the wall John climbed carefully up.

Swallowdale

Horseshoe Cove

At the very end of the northern of the two headlands that made the narrow entrance to the cove, a large towel was waving on the top of an oar fixed to the rocks.

Swallowdale

Kanchenjunga

"That's the hill above the valley the Amazon river comes from," said John. "I've seen it on the map. It's name is . . ."
"Let's have it for Kanchenjunga," said Titty.

Swallowdale

Trout Tarn

Trout Tarn was nearly a mile beyond Swallowdale, high on the top of the moor, a little lake lying in a hollow of rock and heather. When the Swallows saw it, they almost wished that they had made their camp on its rocky shore.

Swallowdale

Waterfall on Kanchenjunga

The stream hurrying down from Kanchenjunga dropped sometimes ten, sometimes twenty feet at a time into pools from which the white foam spirted high in the air to meet it.

Swallowdale

Summit cairn

The box was closed and pushed far back into the hole at the foot of the cairn. Roger wedged the loose stone firmly into place.

Swallowdale

The Path to the Summit

"I'll carry the rope," said Nancy. "We used it all right coming up. I don't see why we shouldn't use the path going down. It'll be lots quicker."

Swallowdale

From the Roof of the World

It was not until that last rush to the top, not until they were actually standing by the cairn that marked the highest point of Kanchenjunga, they they could see what lay beyond the mountain. Then indeed they knew that they were on the roof of the world.

Swallowdale

(The magnificent precipice of Dow Crag from the summit of Coniston Old Man).

The Wigwam

He looked at the hut. It looked newly built, not like the old hut they had seen last year when they had left ***Swallow*** *and climbed through the woods to see the charcoal burners and their smoke. But he could not be sure. The moss that had been pushed between the logs to keep out the rain was still green, but perhaps it was an old hut with new moss on it. "It's a very good wigwam, anyway," said Roger to himself, almost as if it was his own.*

Swallowdale

The Amazon Boathouse

The canoe (which was really the Beckfoot rowing boat) slid into the dark boathouse where the ***Amazon*** *lay moored.*

Swallowdale

Behind Long Island

The wind was driving clear down the narrower channel between the islands and the western side of the lake.

Swallowdale

Dixon's Farm

Dick and Dorothea came round the house and out into the road between the garden and a huge barn.

Winter Holiday

Holly Howe

And down there, between the road and the lake, was a white farmhouse and some outbuildings, not far above what seemed to be a narrow bay.

Winter Holiday

The Igloo

. . . a low hut with no windows, looking almost like a heap of stones.

Winter Holiday

The North Pole

It could not be all windows. He found steps and a door. He hammered on it. There was no answer. He turned the handle, the door opened inwards, and he almost fell through it into a small room.

Winter Holiday

(The lack of quality of the picture is explained by the fact that it is a print from a frame of 8mm colour cine film — all I had with me when I saw the conservatory which was demolished some twenty years ago).

Rio Bay

There was a new world. Everything was white, and somehow still. Everything was holding its breath.

Winter Holiday

(Photo: Michael Wilson)

The Head of the Lake

They trudged on past dim white shores, deep in drifted snow that seemed continually to bear away to the left. They were working round the head of the lake.

Winter Holiday

(Photo: Michael Wilson)

Five Miles to go

It had been a long day's journey from the south, but the last few minutes of it were going like seconds. Already they were in the hill country where walls of loose stones divided field from field. Grey rocks showed through the withered grass. Grey and purple fells lifted to the skies. Titty and Roger hurried from side to side of the carriage, looking first out of one window and then out of another.

Pigeon Post

A First View of the Lake

"There's the lake!" Titty and Roger cried together.
Far below them, beyond the smoking chimneys of a village, glittering water stretched between the hills.

Pigeon Post

The Railway Station

A smallish, ancient motor car with badly dinted mudguards had driven into the station yard.

Pigeon Post

Rio

Mrs Blackett, who had somehow got to the wrong side of the road, swerved back and straightened again. They were coming down the last steep drop into the little village that the Walkers and Blacketts called Rio.

Pigeon Post

The Upper Reaches of the Amazon

Their own road was narrow and winding, going up the valley close to the dried-up little river. Sometimes it almost touched the river bank, and then it would turn suddenly away to climb round a lump of rock only to drop steeply on the other side till it met the river once more.

Pigeon Post

Slater Bob's Mine

A thin trickle of water ran along a winding gutter by a narrow railway track. There was just room for them to step round a four-wheeled trolley.

Pigeon Post

(This narrow railway track is in the main quarry on Coniston Old Man).

Slater Bob's Mine

And then, turning a corner between the high walls built up on either side of them, they saw the narrow railway line disappear into a black hole in the rock. "Hand out the candles, John," said Nancy. "One for everybody".

Pigeon Post

Slater Bob's Mine

Two minutes later they were leaving the outworks of the old mine, coming out between piles of rough stones and dropping down the track to the valley.

Pigeon Post

Old Charcoal Burners' Pitstead

John and Susan had seen the place the day before. Peggy had seen it long ago. Dick, Dorothea, Titty and Roger were seeing it for the first time. It was a round, level platform. Anybody could see that it had been levelled on purpose. One side of it had been built up from below. The other had been levelled by scooping away rock and earth out of the steep side of the hill.

Pigeon Post

High Topps

"Well, what do you think of it?" said Nancy, waving her arm as if she had somehow herself conjured the whole of High Topps into existence.

Pigeon Post

High Topps

*"High Topps is a whacking big place," said John.
They looked out over the rolling fell, all grey rock and dry withered grass, and dusty bracken, with here and there a patch of purple heather.*

Pigeon Post

Among the old Copper Mines

Just the sort of place that even Captain Nancy had said was not particularly safe.

Pigeon Post

Grey Screes

All afternoon Squashy Hat was moving slowly about on the steep slopes of Grey Screes. For a long time even Nancy began to doubt whether he was indeed prospecting. Why, when the gold was somewhere on the Topps should Squashy Hat clamber about those rocky slopes?

Pigeon Post

Rio Bay

At the steamer pier they left the bus, and Timothy carried the suitcases out along one of the landing stages. Two boats were tied up there. One was the ***Amazon,*** *with her Jolly Roger fluttering from her masthead. The other was the old grey rowing boat that usually lay against fenders alongside Captain Flint's houseboat.*

The Picts and the Martyrs

The Hill Country and the Lake

There was the distant peak of Kanchenjunga. Somewhere behind the nearer hills to the south of the great peak lay High Topps where they had been prospectors, found copper, and ended by fighting a fell fire. No matter where they looked, there was always something to remind them of the adventures of the past.

The Picts and the Martyrs

The Amazon River

Foot by foot, yard by yard, they were coming nearer to the deep bank of tall reeds at the edge of the lagoon. There was a little open water between the last of the waterlilies and the reeds. The boat slipped forward and then stopped.

The Picts and the Martyrs

Bridge over the Amazon

Jacky crossed to the other side of the bridge and hove himself up so that he lay with his stomach on the parapet. "There's a big yin down yonder."

The Picts and the Martyrs

A Steamer

The steamer, with a great flurry of reversed propellors, was coming alongside the pier.

The Picts and the Martyrs

The River at the head of the Lake

Dick, as nearly as he could, steered up the middle of the river. The reeds came to an end. There were high earth banks now, and fields with grazing cows.

The Picts and the Martyrs

Beckfoot

But as the house came into sight behind its new-cut lawn, neither of them could help taking just a glance at the scene of last night's burglary.

The Picts and the Martyrs

The Lake looking north

Far up the lake were two white sails waiting for a breath of wind. Beyond them the great hills they had seen from far away towered into the evening sky. "Talk about Wroxham Broad," gasped Pete. "That beat Breydon," said Bill.

Coots in the North

The Secret Harbour: The harbour on Wild Cat Island has become a place of pilgrimage for Ransomites. Brigit Sanders lands a party of explorers from her dinghy *Chick* in August 1987.

Looking for Arthur Ransome's Lakeland Today

Many visitors to the Lake Country drive, as I do, up the M6 from the south. Coming this way you can glimpse the mountains across Morecambe Bay and an experienced eye can pick out Kanchenjunga before entering the National Park. The road by-passes Kendal and Oxenholme (Strickland Junction) but crosses the railway that once carried expresses from London, now reduced to a single line, just before Staveley. As the road reached the last brow of the hill before Windermere town you catch the first sight of the lake, just as Titty and Roger did in *Pigeon Post*. Just below to the left is the railway station, now turned into a supermarket. Above it is the house where Arthur's Aunt Susan used to live when he visited on Sundays while at the Old College. The road to the lake turns left past the shops. Take care not to stray to the wrong side as Mrs. Blackett did, as the traffic is invariably busy. The road to Rio is a pleasant one, full of expectation, and in half a mile the Rio shops appear. These seem to cater for the needs of tourists almost exclusively. Ransome enthusiasts will, hopefully, be able to avoid the months of July and August, when pedestrians spill off narrow pavements on to roads throbbing with traffic.

The bay is still a special place and it is at its best in the early morning and in the evening when the crowds are missing. It is, perhaps, better not to notice Aquarius. It is not easy to imagine those green Victorian boatsheds now, unless one looks at their tiny counterparts near the Old England where it once said "John Walker". Rows of rowing boats still crowd the wooden boat piers and it is very tempting to hire one and "windmill about", as Dick so scornfully thought of it, for it is only from a small boat that the sheer size of Windermere can be fully appreciated.

Many Ransome lovers must have looked across the water from the deck of one of the steamers, eagerly searching for Wild Cat Island. The *Tern* is still in service, clearly recognisable from one of Clifford Webb's illustrations for the early editions of *Swallows and Amazons*. She was built in 1890, having carried thousands of passengers up and down the lake since Arthur was at school in Windermere. The easiest way to see Cormorant Island and Blake Holme is from one of the steamers on its way to Lakeside.

Just north of Bowness Bay is the Windermere Steamboat Museum where a unique collection of steam yachts and other interesting old craft has been brought together. These and the displays give an insight into Victorian and Edwardian life in the area. By one of the specially constructed piers the *Esperance* rocks gently at her moorings. Apart from her place in the stories she has an interesting history. She was built on the Clyde of the finest iron for H.W. Schneider, who had just bought the Belsfield at the back of Bowness Bay. In 1869 she was brought to Lakeside by railway and was used daily by Mr. Schneider to commute to his ironworks at Barrow. Each morning he breakfasted in the cabin while being taken to his waiting train at Lakeside station. In 1941 she sank in 20 feet of water near Blakeholme, but was successfully salvaged a short while later by T.C. Pattinson and moored in the bay where I had first seen her.

The Abbot Hall Museum of Lakeland Life and Industry has a treasure trove of Ransome relics which have recently been re-housed in a room which has the feel of a homely study. Of particular interest are his flags. There is the Jolly Roger made by Evgenia for piratical activities on the Norfolk Broads and his "Swallow" and "Scarab" flags. His desk, souvenirs and pictures and some of his books are on display. Arthur was a great book-collector and this collec-

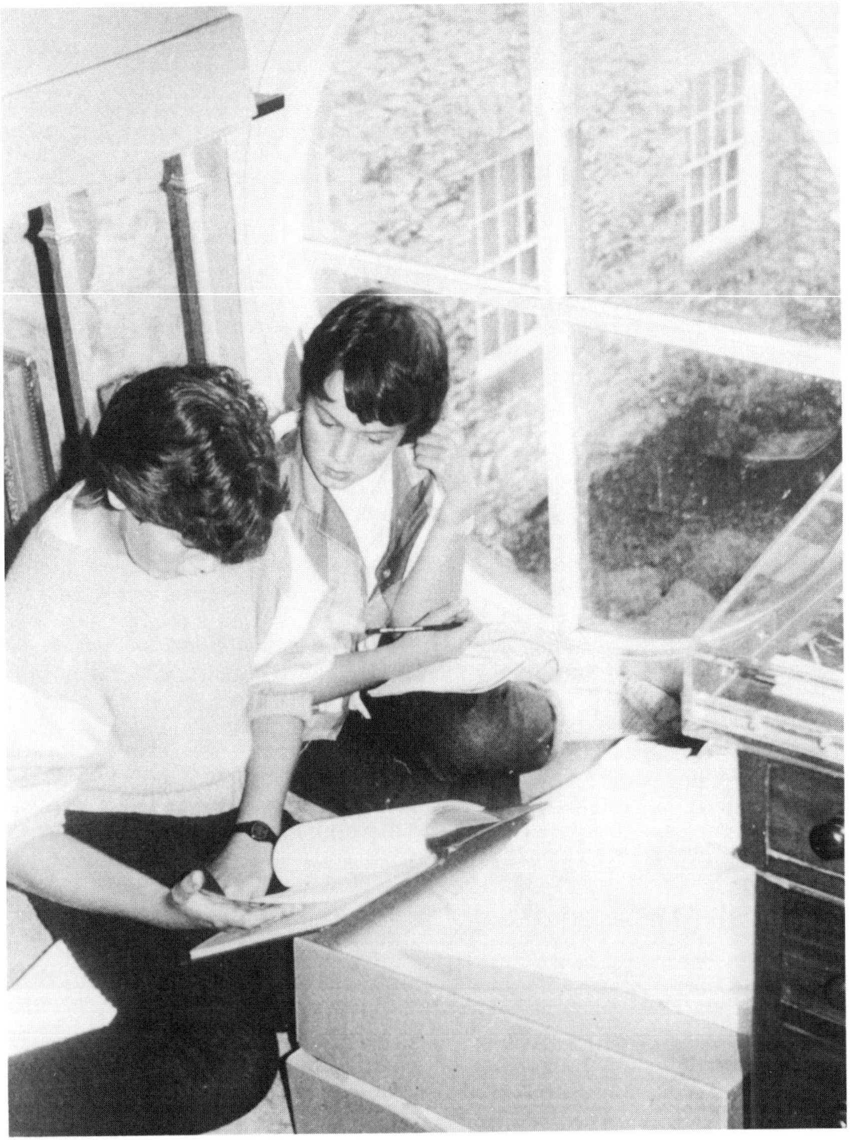

Among the treasures of Abbot Hall not on public show are some of the original typescripts including *Swallows and Amazons* and the unfinished *Coots in the North,* and several sketchbooks, each safely wrapped in tissue paper.

Some favourite pictures and a bust overlook Arthur Ransome's desk and chair. On the top of the desk are momentoes from his travels which he liked to have at hand.

tion, given together with the other items after his death by Genia, is a fascinating one. His first editions, some with his remarks added, together with his favourite books occupy a large bookcase which also holds some charming little model boats made by admirers.

The museum also holds his other flags and the typed drafts for *Swallows and Amazons* and *Coots in the North*. I spent a happy morning here browsing through his sketchbooks and reading *Coots in the North*. Assuming his sketchbooks contain his work alone, then he was a rather more accomplished artist than he has been given credit for.

Anyone driving to Low Ludderburn must be prepared for some steep and narrow roads. It lies on a bend: a tiny whitewashed cottage hiding behind yew trees. There is a lay-by a short distance up the road to the north. From the fell just behind the cottage it is possible to look across the valley to Whitbarrow Scar and beyond. Whatever short-comings the cottage may have had as a home, it has a magnificent outlook. Helen Caldwell showed me into the cottage with its low beams, thick walls and small windows. She took me up some slate steps, where both the Ransomes had accidents, to the barn. The upper room extends the full length of the barn. It has a polished wooden floor, which they had put in when the barn was converted. She showed me bottles of stomach powder, a fragment of Russian type from a typewriter and a part of a clay pipe which had been found on the rubbish dump. On the end of the barn is the garage they added for their car. It features on the decorative border of the card he used for replying to his admirers.

It is only a short drive from Low Ludderburn to the car park at Gummers How. From its summit there is a panoramic view from the Pennines, over Morecambe Bay, and round to the Coniston Fells. A few yards from the summit towards the lake it is possible to see the spectacular view of almost the whole of Windermere. It is a grand view of the Ransome country.

Kanchenjunga is a magnificent mountain. Aircraft have crashed into it, miners have driven holes deep into it, quarrymen have disfigured parts of it and tourists are wearing it away along the popular routes, but it remains one of the finest mountains in the Lake District. It towers over Coniston village, its features sharply revealed on some days and obscured by cloud on others. As it stands on the southern end of the mountain ridge which form the Coniston Fells, its best aspect is from the south where it resembles a shapely cone.

My favourite route follows the ravine of Church Beck into the wild Coppermines Valley. Beyond the Youth Hostel is a possible site for the Swallow's half-way camp. The path slopes upwards towards Levers Water, but I branch left across a wooden footbridge by a couple of copper mine levels. From here it is a level walk to Boulder Valley where I cut right up into the heart of the spoil heaps of the main quarry. Here is the area of Slater Bob's quarry, as the path winds through spoil heaps, cables long-since fallen and a mine entrance or two. It is a relief to come out of the slate and see the startling blue water of Low Water Tarn.

From here the summit is clearly visible eight hundred feet higher, curving round to Brimfell where Roger saw wild goats. The wild goats have long gone but I have met some very tame sheep on the highest point. From Low Water the path zig-zags up to the top of the Ling Scar ridge and then follows the ridge a short distance to the summit. This last part is becoming badly eroded. The view from the summit is terrific. It is different whichever way you look. To the south is the shining water of Morecambe Bay. West is the breathtaking cliff of Dow Crag. North is the highest land in England: the Scafells, and north-east is a spectacular view of Low Water. Further east is the full length of Coniston Water.

I like to descend by Goats Water and across to the Walna Scar Road. This is not High Topps, but the area where it was placed in relation to Kanchenjunga.

Slater Bob's mine can be found a short distance from the car park by the bridge at Tilberthwaite. Eric Holland's book *Coniston Copper Mines* gives details of the quarry in Horse Crag Level where Squashy Hat repeated the legend of the gold. The level used to run through to Tilberthwaite mine more than half a mile away. This became the Old Level in *Pigeon Post*. Follow the path up the south side of Tilberthwaite Gill, and under the shadow of Weatherlam is High Topps. It is fine wild country to explore, but a word of caution. *Pigeon Post* gives a very accurate picture of the area and warns against going into any of the levels, but it does not mention any of the vertical shafts which are not fenced off and very dangerous. Future explorers are

A Swallow and the *Amazon*.
Brigit Sanders with *Mavis* by their boathouse at Nibthwaite, Coniston.

warned to keep their dogs on a lead and not to let young children wander.

The Holly Howe boathouse can be seen from the road on the opposite shore of Coniston Water. The road goes round the head of the lake and down the east side. It is charming and full of interest to Ransomites. Even these days it is fairly quiet and there are several parking places. Not far down is Tent Lodge and around the next bend we come to Lanehead. The copper beech Taqui remembers from her childhood still stands by the road, but the house no longer seems like anyone's home, being an outdoor pursuits centre. Here it was that W.G. Collingwood and his family welcomed Arthur and allowed him to share their life. It was the home of various members of the family until about twenty years ago.

Holly Howe is just a field away and may be reached by a public footpath passing near the farm. It is still possible to stay there, just as the Walkers did. A mile further on is Brantwood, Ruskin's home, which is open to the public. Here they occasionally hold a Charcoal Burner's Fayre and fortunately my visit last August coincided with one and I was able to take a couple of photographs.

The road runs close to the shore in places and by the broadleaved woodlands which are such a feature of this side of the lake. The scene is at its best in autumn when the gold of the leaves and the blue of water and sky make an unforgettable sight.

A little way back from the road is the bungalow, The Heald. Like other Ransome houses it has a wonderful outlook, but it is really miles from anywhere. About half a mile further on, in the steep woods leading up from the road, are dozens of charcoal pitsteads and several charcoal burners' hut sites. Exploring these woods some years ago I found the ruin of a stone building which fitted the description of the igloo. South of Lanehead, in the steep woodland leading down to the road explorers may come across a hut they will recognise as The Dog's Home.

Wild Cat Island can be seen from some distance away and, although it is not visible from the road when the island is reached, it is easy to walk through the National Trust land to the shore which has a good view of the landing and the harbour. Nearby is the cliff which may have inspired the Peak in Darian.

A mile to the south is the tiny community of High Nibthwaite where Brigit and her husand John Sanders have made their home. There is very little space to park a car here, but the hamlet should be explored on foot. Here beneath the bridge over the beck Arthur tickled trout, and a few yards away a farm track leads to Swainson's Farm and through the gate a path goes to Bethecar. A short way along the path a group of rocks was given the name "The Gondola" and was one of Arthur's favourite lookouts. From here there is a good view over Nibthwaite to the lagoon and the boathouse where *Amazon* is moored. Not far away is the knickerbockerbreaker and a pleasant fell walk leads to the Top o' Selside which offers an extensive view over the lake to the Coniston Fells.

A footpath from Bouthray Bridge, Water Yeat follows the River Amazon for a short distance and passes near Octopus Lagoon. This reed-fringed tarn is dotted with water lilies and is about a hundred metres across. It is one of the most instantly recognisable of the Ransome places.

A short distance from the foot of the lake an inlet in the western shore is the original Horseshoe Cove. The northern cape can be recognised from an illustration by Clifford Webb, who was very accurate with topographic detail. A beck flows into the bay and it is a convenient picnic spot from Nibthwaite.

Trout Tarn is one of the loveliest of the lowland tarns and is visited by many people who have no idea of its association with *Swallowdale*. It lies to the south of Beacon Fell, one of my favourite lower summitis which should be visited on any expedition to Trout Tarn.

Swallowdale is an enchanting spot. It was fashioned during the ice age when a glacier ground a splendid miniature U-shaped valley among the fells by Coniston Water. It lies somewhere in the triangle bounded by the A593, A5084 and A5092 roads. It would be unfair to deprive the reader the satisfaction of discovery by letting out any more secrets. A young reader who had explored the valley more thoroughly than I, wrote to tell me she had found a cleft between two rocks like a tiny cave. It is rather small, but quite enough for an imaginative child to remember and improve in a story, forty years on. The waterfall and valley itself look rather more like Clifford Webb's illustrations for the first edition than they do

Arthur's own drawn several years later, which look more like Mitredale — a site suggested by several people including Arthur's grandson in America. No footpath leads to Swallowdale, the bracken which covers the valley floor shows no sign of having been disturbed, and the only sound is the bubbling gurgle of the waterfalls. "The only way to keep a secret . . ."

Years ago I looked at the site of Oxen House when searching for Beckfoot, but was put off, as others have been, by the appearance of the house: so unlike the square building of the illustrations. However, everything else is just right: it lies at the foot of Torver Beck, there is a stable block adjacent, the road passes close by and across the lawn there is a boathouse. In the 1920's the interior of the house bore some resemblance to Beckfoot with the front door at the opposite end of the building from the kitchen, while a passage led to the pantry for the pigeon bell to be fastened. In the last fifty years the building has been extensively altered inside and out, and so has the stable block across the yard. The boathouse has silted up in spite of the efforts of Professor Constantinesco, a remarkable inventor who owned Oxen House for a number of years. Several attempts to dredge it have ended in failure and there it stands on the shore, empty and rather forlorn. When writing Swallows and Amazons, I suspect Arthur moved it into the river to lead the Swallows towards the fun of Octopus Lagoon. Future explorers are warned to keep well away from Torver Beck which is not navigable.

Unless you bring your own boat to Coniston, the only way I know to voyage to Wild Cat Island is to hire a rowing boat from the boat landing near the village and row. It is a pleasant old-fashioned way of travel and on a still, warm day the seven miles round trip is not arduous and is a pleasure in itself. If you have to pull back to the village against a strong wind, however, it is a very different matter, so do choose your day with care. When you circumnavigate Wild Cat Island, be like Roger and keep a sharp look out for reddish rocks under the water. The landing place is suitable for beaching a rowing boat, but most people make for one of the harbours unless they are over-crowded. There are two harbours at the southern end of the island, either side of a very large rock, but the western one is more sheltered. The island is in the care of the National Trust and there are notices which say "No Fires" and "No Camping". In spite of many visitors it is quite unspoiled and as full of charm as it ever was.

The setting of the stories is the traditional Lake District of yesterday, woven from features of the area and topographic fragments which Arthur knew. Nevertheless explorers will still find it whenever they leave the crowds behind and drift along in a boat or wander over the fells and through the woods as he did.

Bibliography

Altounyan, Taqui, *In Aleppo Once* (John Murray, 1969).

Brogan, Hugh *The Life of Arthur Ransome* (Jonathan Cape, 1984).

Collingwood, William *The Lake Counties* (Dent, 1902; revised edition 1932).

Hardyment, Christina *Arthur Ransome and Captain Flint's Trunk* (Jonathan Cape, 1984).

Holland, Eric *Coniston Copper Mines: A Field Guide* (Cicerone Press, 1981).

Ransome, Arthur *Swallows and Amazons* (Jonathan Cape, 1930).

Swallows and Amazons (Illustrated by Clifford Webb, 1931).

Swallows and Amazons (Illustrated by the author, 1938).

Swallowdale (Illustrated by Clifford Webb, Jonathan Cape, 1931).

Swallowdale (Illustrated by the author, 1936).

Winter Holiday (Jonathan Cape, 1933).

Pigeon Post (Jonathan Cape, 1936).

Picts and the Martyrs (Jonathan Cape, 1943).

Coots in the North (Unfinished typescript, Abbot Hall, Kendal).

Autobiography (Edited and with prologue and epilogue by Rupert Hart-Davis, Jonathan Cape, 1976).

Wainwright, Alfred *The Southern Fells* (Westmorland Gazette, 1960).

The Outlying Fells of Lakeland (Westmorland Gazette, 1974).

Afloat on Coniston Water 1985

More than ninety years since Arthur Ransome first sailed on the lake a great, great grandson of W.G. Collingwood sits in the bows of the native war canoe with other members of the family while visitors from the south set out aboard *Amazon* from Nibthwaite.

Acknowledgements

Without exception everyone I approached in the production of this book has been kind and helpful, which has not only simplified matters but has made it such a pleasurable undertaking.

Firstly I would like to thank Arthur Ransome's executors for allowing me to make use of the extracts from the *Swallows and Amazons* books which accompany most of the photographs. My thanks are also due to Anthony Colwell of Jonathan Cape, Ransome's publisher, for his help.

I received nothing but encouragement from the Altounyan family. Mrs. Taqui Stephens read the greater part of the text to check its accuracy, Mrs. Brigit Sanders let me use some photographs she had taken and the late Dr. Roger Altounyan and Mr. Tadeus Altounyan told me the story of "Mavis".

I have to thank Miss Mary Birkett O.B.E., Director of Abbot Hall Museum of Lakeland Life and Industry, who gave me the run of the Ransome room and allowed me to use three photographs I took there. Mrs. C. Trelogan was most helpful during my visit. Mrs. Ann Farr has charge of the Ransome collection at the Brotherton Library at the University of Leeds and she very kindly looked out the photograph of *Swallow* for me.

Mrs. Helen Caldwell welcomed me to Low Ludderburn and Mrs. Sheila Caldwell showed me over the Barkbooth barn. I have to thank Mr. Michael Wilson for lending me his negatives and Mr. Des Berry for seeking out the sort of photographs I wanted. I am grateful to Christina Hardyment for pointing me towards Swallowdale after a correspondent of hers had shared the secret.

Mrs. Angela Fox wrote to say "I think I live at Beckfoot. Come and see," and I am very grateful to her for this and for allowing me to explore so thoroughly. Richard Litton lived at Oxen House for a number of years and he told me of the many changes to the house. Other Ransome enthusiasts who let me into their secrets were Mr. John Berry who found The Dog's Home and Brigit Low, the discoverer of the "very small cave" in Swallowdale.

Finally I would like to thank Matthew and Emma Cornwall and Caroline Barton, explorers in the true Swallows tradition, who came with me to most of the places in the books and made it so much fun.